GW01375224

& Spores.

ALS No. B38 2089692

This item should be returned on or before the last date stamped above. If not in demand it may be renewed for a further period by personal application, by telephone, or in writing. The author, title, above number and date due back should be quoted.   LS/3

## ALL WAYS OF LOOKING AT

# SEEDS, BULBS AND SPORES

### Jane Walker

**GLOUCESTER PRESS**
LONDON • NEW YORK • SYDNEY

# INTRODUCTION

Did you know that there are hundreds of thousands of types of plants in the world? All of them survive by multiplying. Some grow bulbs underground, and others shed spores into the air. Most, however, produce seeds.

In this book we show you the wonderful ways plants reproduce. You can have fun with a number of **Practical Projects**, and we tell you how to write your own **Nature Diary**. Discover also a lot of **Amazing Facts** about seeds, bulbs and spores.

© Aladdin Books Ltd 1993

Designed and produced by
Aladdin Books Ltd
28 Percy Street
London W1P 9FF

First published in
Great Britain in 1993 by
WATTS BOOKS
96 Leonard Street
London EC2A 4RH

Design:       David West
              Children's Book
              Design
Designer:     Flick Killerby
Cartoons:     Tony Kenyon
Illustrators: Caroline Barnard,
              Justine Peek
Consultant:   Joyce Pope

ISBN 0 7496 1318 1

Printed in Belgium
All rights reserved

A CIP catalogue record for this book is available from the British Library

Kingston upon Hull City Libraries
Group SCHOOLS
Class 582
ISBN
ALS No. B382089692

# CONTENTS

- SEEDS, BULBS AND SPORES ........................ 4
  The Roman myth of the seasons
- ALL KINDS OF SEEDS ................................. 6
  Making a seed picture
- WATCHING SEEDS GROW ........................... 8
  Growing beans
- HOW DO SEEDS DEVELOP? ....................... 10
  Looking for pollen
- FROM FLOWERS TO FRUIT ....................... 12
  Making fruit and nut jewellery
- HOW SEEDS TRAVEL ................................ 14
  The Pilgrim Fathers
- SEEDS AS FOOD ....................................... 16
  Early farmers
- BULBS AND CORMS ................................. 18
  Making onion skin dye
- TUBERS, RHIZOMES AND RUNNERS .......... 20
  A potato maze
- PLANTS WITHOUT FLOWERS .................... 22
  Growing mould
- FROM SPORES TO NEW PLANTS ............... 24
  Finding fossils
- PLANT FAMILIES ..................................... 26
- KEEPING A RECORD ................................ 28
- MORE AMAZING FACTS ........................... 30
- GLOSSARY .............................................. 31
- INDEX .................................................... 32

# SEEDS, BULBS & SPORES

*MOSS plants release their spores.*

## Spores

Some plants do not have flowers, so they cannot make seeds. These non–flowering plants include ferns, mosses, algae, fungi and lichens. Instead of seeds, they release tiny single cells, called spores.

All plants can make more of their own kind. Most plants that grow on land produce seeds, which will grow into new plants. Some plants, however, grow from special underground parts each year, while other plants make tiny spores, from which new plants will grow.

*SWEET CHESTNUT TREE*

## Seeds and fruits

Most of the plants that you see around you, like marigolds or oak trees, are called flowering plants. They all grow flowers, which later produce the plants' seeds. A part of each flower may develop into a fruit, which protects the seeds inside it. Some fruits, like raspberries and tomatoes, are soft and fleshy. But fruits like acorns and other nuts are hard, with a strong outer shell.

*The seeds of a SWEET CHESTNUT tree are reddish–brown nuts. Each nut is protected by a spiny case.*

*The largest seed in the world comes from the COCO DE MER tree. One nut can weigh over 20 kilograms.*

## Bulbs

Some flowering plants, like onions and daffodils, have special underground parts called bulbs. A bulb is made of layers of leaves wrapped around a small stem. The plant stores food inside the bulb. Each spring, new flowers and leaves grow from the bulb. Small bulbs growing from the side of the main bulb make new plants.

*ONIONS are bulbs that we can eat.*

*BRAZIL NUTS are seeds that have hard outer shells to protect them.*

*Some FERNS develop spores on the back of their fronds, or leaves.*

## The Roman myth of the seasons

Ceres was the goddess of farming. Her daughter Proserpine was kidnapped by Pluto, the god of the underworld. Proserpine ate some pomegranate seeds – a symbol of marriage – and became his wife. However, she returned for part of each year. During her visits, Ceres was happy and made the land warm and sunny.

*Pomegranate*

# ALL KINDS OF SEEDS

*Tomato*

Plants that produce seeds are divided into two groups. All flowering plants, including flowering trees and shrubs, belong to one group. Their seeds are covered, or enclosed, in a fruit. The other group includes only those trees and shrubs whose seeds are not in pods or fruits, so they are uncovered, or naked.

### Fading flowers
When a plant has finished flowering, its flower petals fade and die. The hollow part at the bottom of the flower starts to swell. It slowly forms a fruit. Inside are egg cells which develop into seeds.

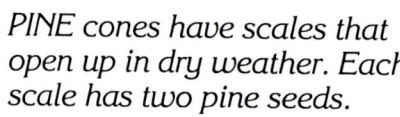

*PINE cones have scales that open up in dry weather. Each scale has two pine seeds.*

### Naked seeds
Most of the plants that produce naked seeds are conifers. Conifers are trees and shrubs that produce cones. The hard cones are made up of scales. The conifer seeds develop on these scales. When the scales open up, the seeds are released.

6

*The world's smallest seeds are produced by ORCHID plants.*

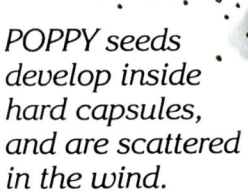

*POPPY seeds develop inside hard capsules, and are scattered in the wind.*

## Enclosed seeds

The seeds of flowering plants are enclosed in pods, capsules, or fruits. The number of seeds a plant makes depends on the size of the seed. Some plants, like coconut trees, grow only a few large, heavy seeds. Others, like orchids, produce thousands of light, tiny seeds. Fruits like cherries and plums have a single seed inside a hard stone. Other fruits, like melons and bananas, contain lots of seeds surrounded by soft fruit.

## Making a seed picture

Make a collection of as many different seeds as you can find. To make a seed picture, first draw an outline on a sheet of plain paper or card. Use a gluestick to stick on your seeds. Poppy, melon and sunflower seeds, sesame seeds, rice and dried kidney beans are just some of the seeds you could use.

# WATCHING SEEDS GROW

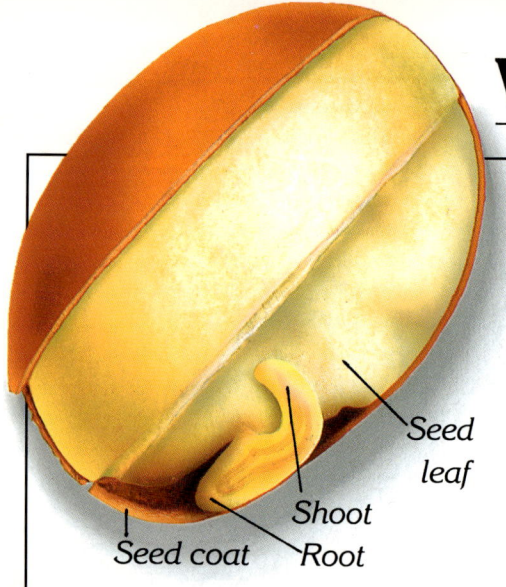

Inside the hard outer coat of every seed is a tiny new plant. The seed also contains a special store of food, which the tiny plant needs to help it grow. A seed needs two main things before it can begin to grow: water and warmth. The seed shoot will grow towards warm sunlight. The root will grow downwards.

### Inside a seed
The seed coat is a hard outer case that protects the seed. Inside it are the first root, the first shoot and one or two special seed leaves.

*The BEAN starts to grow.*

*The root pushes out and grows downwards.*

*The shoot breaks out through the seed coat and starts to grow upwards.*

### Roots and shoots
When a seed starts growing, water enters the seed. The growing parts of the new plant begin to swell. First, the root breaks through the seed coat and starts to grow downwards. Next, the shoot pushes through and begins to grow upwards. Tiny hairs grow on the root and take in water and minerals from the soil. When the shoot has pushed through the surface of the soil, green leaves appear.

*Seeds of an ARCTIC LUPIN plant grew after lying in the ground for over 10,000 years.*

## Food stores

Some plants, like maize, have only one seed leaf. Others, like broad beans, have two seed leaves. The seed leaves in some seeds store food for the new plant. Inside some seeds, such as cereals and the castor oil plant, is a special food tissue surrounding the tiny plant.

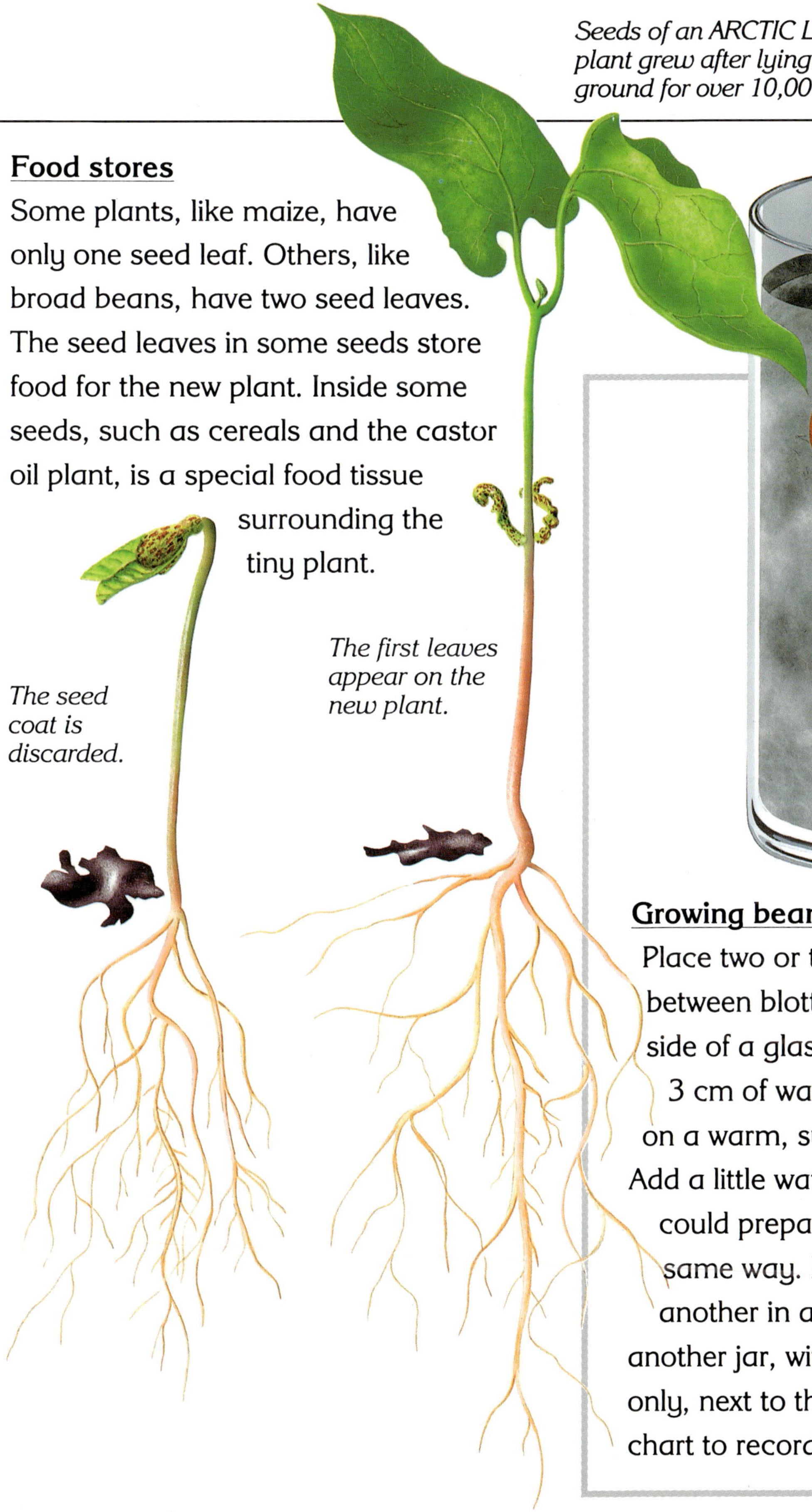

*The seed coat is discarded.*

*The first leaves appear on the new plant.*

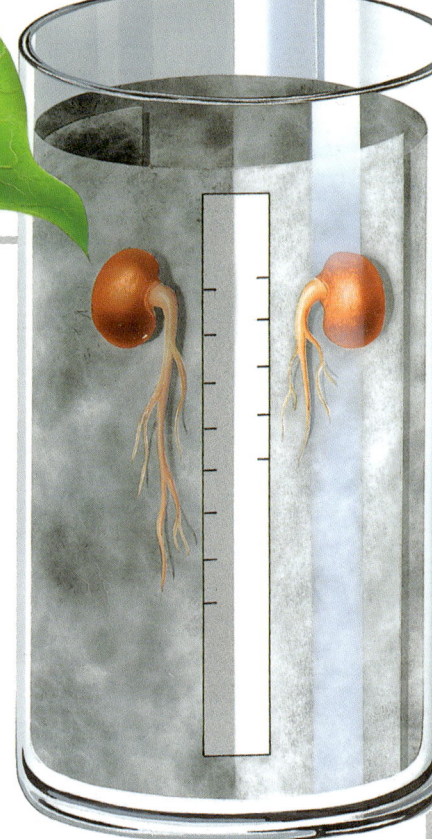

## Growing beans

Place two or three bean seeds between blotting paper and the side of a glass jar. Pour in about 3 cm of water and stand the jar on a warm, sunny window–sill. Add a little water each day. You could prepare more jars in the same way. Put one in a fridge, another in a dark place, and another jar, with paper and seeds only, next to the first jar. Make a chart to record what happens.

# How do seeds develop?

*Male (Stamen)*

*Female (Pistil or carpel)*

**Male and female**
The female part of a flower is called the pistil or carpel. It contains the plant's egg cells. The male parts are called the stamens. They produce the pollen.

All flowering plants produce seeds. The flowers contain the male and female parts that make the seeds. The male part produces pollen, which has to reach the female part. This transfer of pollen is called pollination. After pollination, a pollen grain grows a special tube that reaches down and joins with the female egg cells. These cells then become seeds.

*APPLE BLOSSOM is pollinated by insects such as bees.*

The COMET ORCHID is pollinated by a moth with a 20-cm-long tongue.

## Animal or wind?

Pollen is carried from one flower to another by the wind, by insects, by birds and even by small mammals. Most flowers are pollinated by insects. The bright colours of the flower petals attract insects, which feed on the flower's pollen and a sweet liquid called nectar. As an insect feeds, pollen sticks to its hairy body. When it visits another flower, some pollen brushes off. This is how pollination takes place.

*A bee uses its POLLEN BASKETS to take pollen back to its nest.*

*This pollen grain from a HOLLYHOCK flower is 1,000 times bigger than its true size.*

*Pollen is blown off HAZEL catkins by the wind.*

## Looking for pollen

Some flowers have special markings on their petals called honey guides. They help bees to find the nectar. Take a magnifying glass and if you spot a bee at work, look closely at its legs. You may see yellow clumps, or "baskets", filled with pollen. Be careful, and remember that bees can sting!

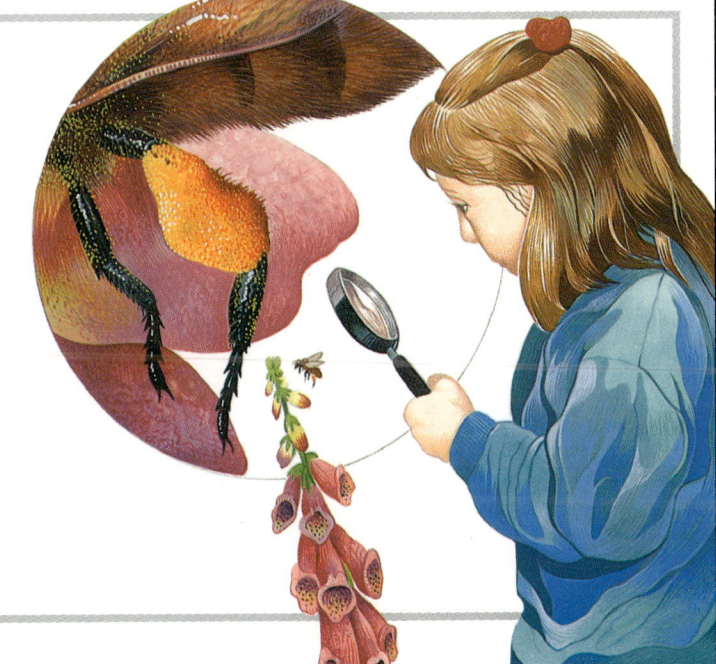

# From Flowers to Fruit

When pollen grains reach a flower's egg cells, they join with, or fertilise, them. Once the egg cells are fertilised, they are ready to grow into seeds. The hollow part at the bottom of the flower soon starts to swell and to form a fruit. It protects the seeds that are developing inside. The seed inside a peach has grown from a single fertilised egg cell.

*Sunflower*

**Tiny flowers**
In the centre of the large head of a sunflower are hundreds of tiny flowers, called florets. Each floret can develop into a seed. The flower head of a thistle plant is also made up of tiny florets. Each one develops into an individual seed that is attached to a feathery "parachute".

*After fertilisation, the outer casing at the base of the APPLE BLOSSOM begins to swell.*

*The petals wither, die and fall to the ground.*

*As it swells up, the fleshy part changes colour and starts to ripen.*

*The CROSSBILL's crossed beak is designed to get seeds from pine cones.*

*HAZEL CATKINS are made up of hundreds of tiny flowers.*

*A leafy casing surrounds each HAZEL NUT.*

## Nuts and cones

Many trees, such as oak and beech trees, develop hard fruits. Each fruit has an outer case, or shell, which protects the nut inside. The nut is the tree's seed. Pine trees and cedar trees do not grow flowers that form fruits. Their female "flowers" slowly develop into hard dry cones. This process can take at least three years in a conifer like a pine. The seeds develop on the scales that make up the cones. Juniper trees are another kind of conifer. Their cones look like juicy berries.

*A HAZEL NUT consists of a hard shell around a single seed.*

## Making fruit and nut jewellery

You can make pretty jewellery with dried fruit and some seeds. Use a large needle and some thin round elastic, and thread it through dried apples, pears, melon seeds, red kidney beans, or horse chestnuts. You may need adult help to make holes in the harder seeds. To make a fastener, you can use paperclips tied onto the ends of the elastic. To preserve your jewellery, you need to paint the fruit with a clear gloss varnish.

# HOW SEEDS TRAVEL

In order to grow into a healthy new plant, a seed must land on good soil, in an open space. Seeds are scattered, or dispersed, in four main ways: by wind, water, animals or by the plant itself. Plants that can spread their seeds themselves have seed heads or pods, which burst open, spilling out the seeds.

### Travel by water
Rivers, streams and the sea carry seeds from plants living in the water or near the water's edge. The fruits of the coconut tree are carried long distances by the sea.

### The Pilgrim Fathers
In 1620, the Pilgrim Fathers sailed from England to America. During their first year, their crops failed and many of them starved. The next year, the Indians gave them corn seeds to plant. Later that year, they held a service to thank God for their crops. Americans still celebrate Thanksgiving Day every November.

*NUTS are carried away by squirrels and jays and stored as food for the winter.*

TUMBLEWEED plants spread their seeds as they blow across the American prairies.

## Help from animals
Birds eat colourful berries. The seeds inside a berry pass right through the bird and out onto the ground, as part of the bird's droppings. The seeds then begin to grow. Fruits like goosegrass stick to the furry bodies of some animals and are carried away from the parent plant. Acorns and nuts are stored by squirrels and jays, as winter food. Any that remain uneaten may grow into new plants.

BURS, which are fruits covered with tiny hooks, stick on a fox's fur.

SYCAMORE SEEDS

LIME SEEDS

DANDELION SEEDS

## Wind dispersal
Some seeds have the right shape for being carried by the wind. Sycamore and ash trees, for example, have seeds with wings. Dandelion seeds are attached to tiny feather–like parachutes, which help to carry them away on the wind. In the late summer and autumn, find as many different seeds as you can. Those with wings or parachutes will probably be some distance away from the plants that released them.

# SEEDS AS FOOD

Bread, pasta, biscuits and margarine are all made from seeds. In every corner of the world, seeds provide food for people and animals. We eat seeds from cereals such as maize, rice and wheat. Peas and beans are also seeds from plants. Seeds also give us drinks, oils and spices.

### Oils
Oils for cooking, such as sunflower oil and corn oil, are made from seeds. We use the oil from the seeds of the yellow rape flower to make margarine.

*WHEAT*

*BARLEY*

*RICE*

*OATS*

### Cereals
Cereals are special kinds of grass plants. Some, like barley, are grown as food for farm animals. Rice is grown in hot countries where there is plenty of rain. Most rice plants grow in fields flooded with water, which are called paddy fields.

*In ancient Egypt, people chewed CARDAMOM seeds to clean their teeth.*

## Drinks

Coffee is made from the dried seeds, or beans, of the coffee plant. Inside each red coffee berry are two white beans. The beans are dried and roasted, when they change to a dark brown colour. The seeds of the cacao tree grow inside pods. The seeds are taken out, dried and then crushed to form a powder – cocoa. The Aztecs from Mexico were the first people to make a hot chocolate drink from cacao seeds.

COFFEE BEANS

CACAO BEANS

*Many of the colourful SPICES on sale in this Indian market are made from crushed seeds.*

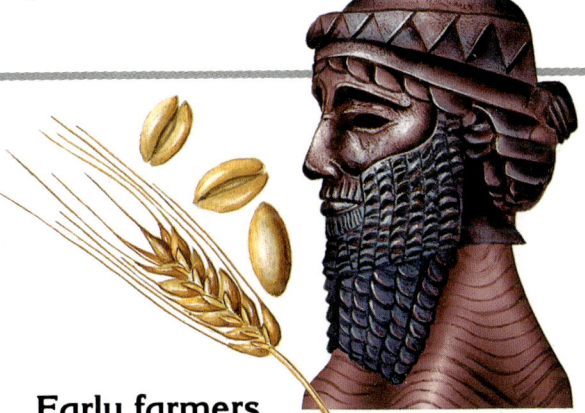

## Early farmers

The Sumerian people were some of the world's earliest farmers. They lived in Mesopotamia (modern Iraq) about 5,500 years ago. The Sumerians grew crops like barley and corn. After each harvest, they kept the very best seeds and replanted them the following spring. In this way, their crops became stronger and better.

# BULBS AND CORMS

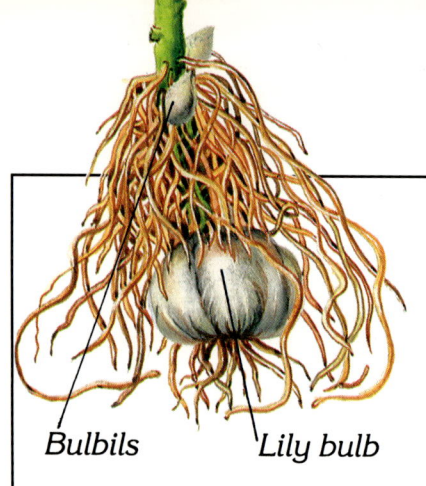

*Bulbils   Lily bulb*

Some plants produce new flowers and leaves each year without the help of seeds. These plants have special underground parts, which store food and water during the growing season. The plant uses this food to stay alive during the winter, and to start growing again the following spring.

### New plants
Lilies and tulips grow from bulbs. Small buds grow from the side of the main bulb. At first, before they are fully grown, they are called bulbils.

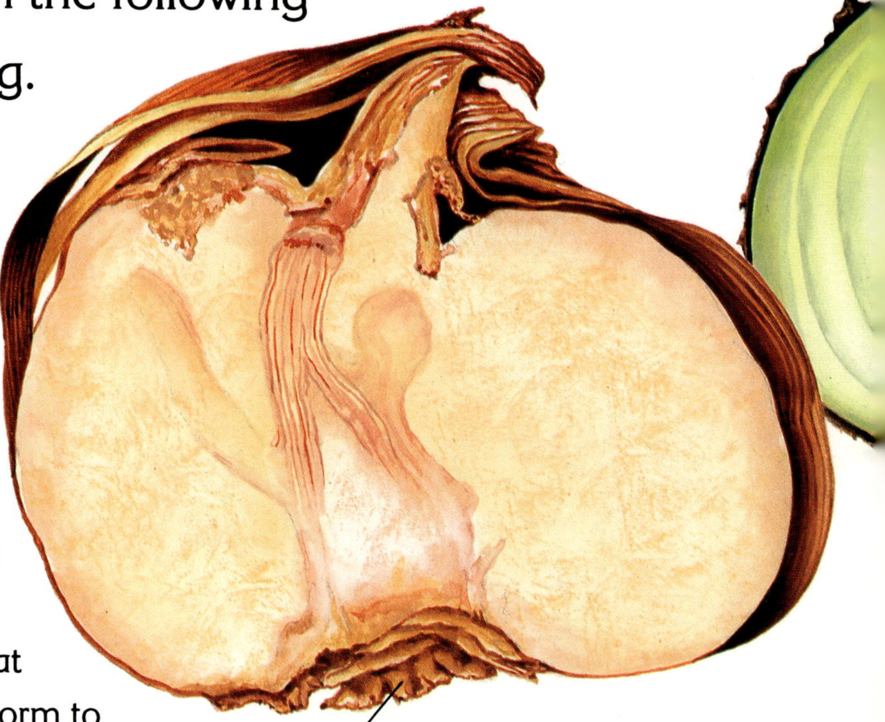

*A GLADIOLUS corm swells as it stores food and water.*

### Corms
A corm is a kind of thickened underground stem. It consists of a single bud which is surrounded by a paper–like skin. The main corm eventually dies, but first it develops at least one new corm to replace itself.

*The new corm is forming. The skin is the remains of the previous year's leaves.*

*GLADIOLUS corm and flower*

*In horror stories, people often carry GARLIC BULBS to protect themselves against vampires.*

## Bulbs

Bulbs consist of layers of thick, fleshy leaves that are wrapped around a central bud. In spring, the stem, leaves and flowers grow up from this underground bud. At the end of the growing season, the growing parts above the ground wither and die, but the underground bulb stays alive. It feeds on the food it has stored in its leaves.

*An ONION bulb has many layers of fleshy leaves that store food and water.*

*Fleshy leaves*

*ONION bulb and flower*

### Making onion skin dye

Did you know that you can make a dye from onion skins? The Vikings used red–skinned onions to make a rich red dye. Ask an adult to help you boil two onions in a saucepan of water. Cook them for 2–3 hours, and allow the pan to cool before removing the onions. Carefully lower material you want to dye into the liquid. Add salt to the dye to help fix the colour. Remove the material and rinse it in cold water.

# TUBERS, RHIZOMES AND RUNNERS

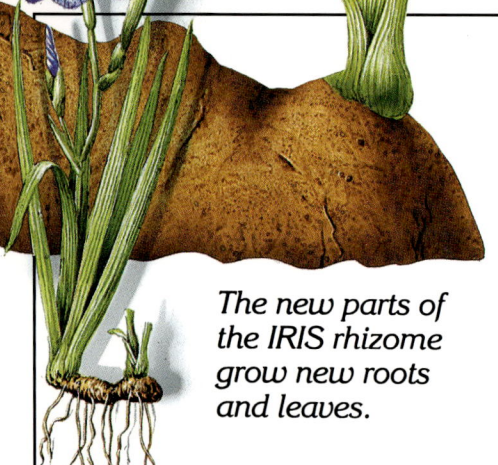

*The new parts of the IRIS rhizome grow new roots and leaves.*

Tubers, rhizomes and runners are parts of adult plants that make new plants without the help of seeds. Like corms (see page 18), tubers and rhizomes are underground stems. Runners are sideways stems that grow out from the parent plant and then grow their own roots.

## Rhizomes

Rhizomes are thick stems which grow along sideways from the main plant. They usually grow underground, or sometimes on the surface.

*STRAWBERRY plants grow new plants on their runners.*

## Runners

Strawberry plants have long stems, called runners, which grow along the ground. The runners develop roots which are the starting point for a new plant. This plant can be cut away from the main plant. The creeping buttercup plant also produces runners in the same way.

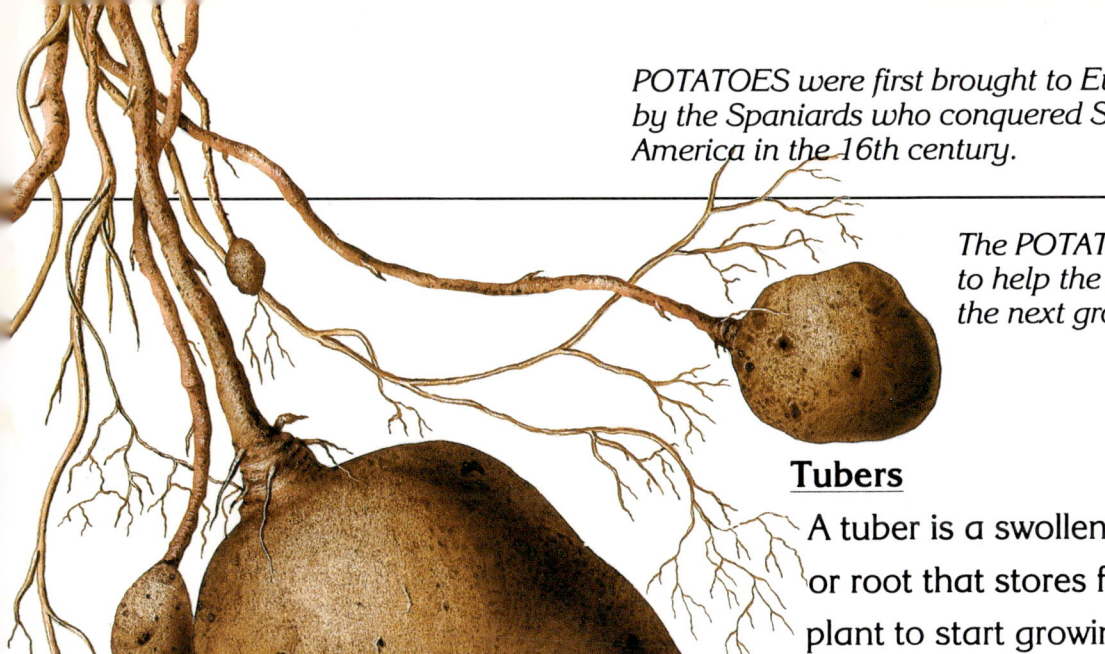

POTATOES were first brought to Europe by the Spaniards who conquered South America in the 16th century.

The POTATO plant stores food to help the plant survive until the next growing season.

## Tubers

A tuber is a swollen underground stem or root that stores food. It helps the plant to start growing again after the cold winter. The dahlia plant is a root tuber. Potatoes are stem tubers. Their buds are called eyes. You can grow several plants from one potato, by cutting it into pieces, each with an eye in it.

## A potato maze

You can see for yourself how a new potato plant starts to grow from an old potato. Place a shoebox on one end. Make some shelves out of stiff card and stick them onto the sides of the shoebox. Cut a small hole out of the top of the box. Find an old potato with at least one eye, and put it in the bottom of the box. Fasten on the lid and stand the box in a cool, well–lit place. The shoot will grow up your maze.

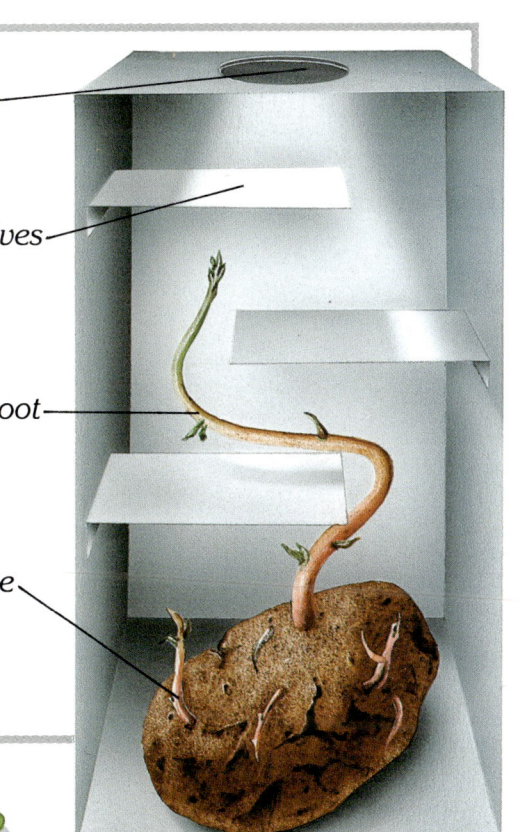

Hole for sunlight

Card shelves to form maze

Potato shoot

Potato eye

21

# Plants without flowers

The first plants that grew on land lived about 400 million years ago. They did not have either flowers or seeds. Many plants like these still survive today. They include algae and fungi, as well as liverworts, mosses, horsetails, club-mosses and ferns. Instead of seeds, the plants produce tiny cells, called spores.

*Algae*

### Algae
Most algae grow in either salty sea-water or freshwater streams and ponds. Some are so tiny that you need a microscope to see them clearly. Seaweeds are the largest kinds of algae. One, the Pacific giant kelp, can grow to over 60 metres long.

*This bright red FLY AGARIC mushroom is very poisonous.*

FAIRY RING MUSHROOM

### Growing mould
Sprinkle water onto a slice of stale bread. Place it in a tin or similar container and put on the lid. After 2–3 days, mould will start to appear on the surface of the bread. Can you see the tiny spores?

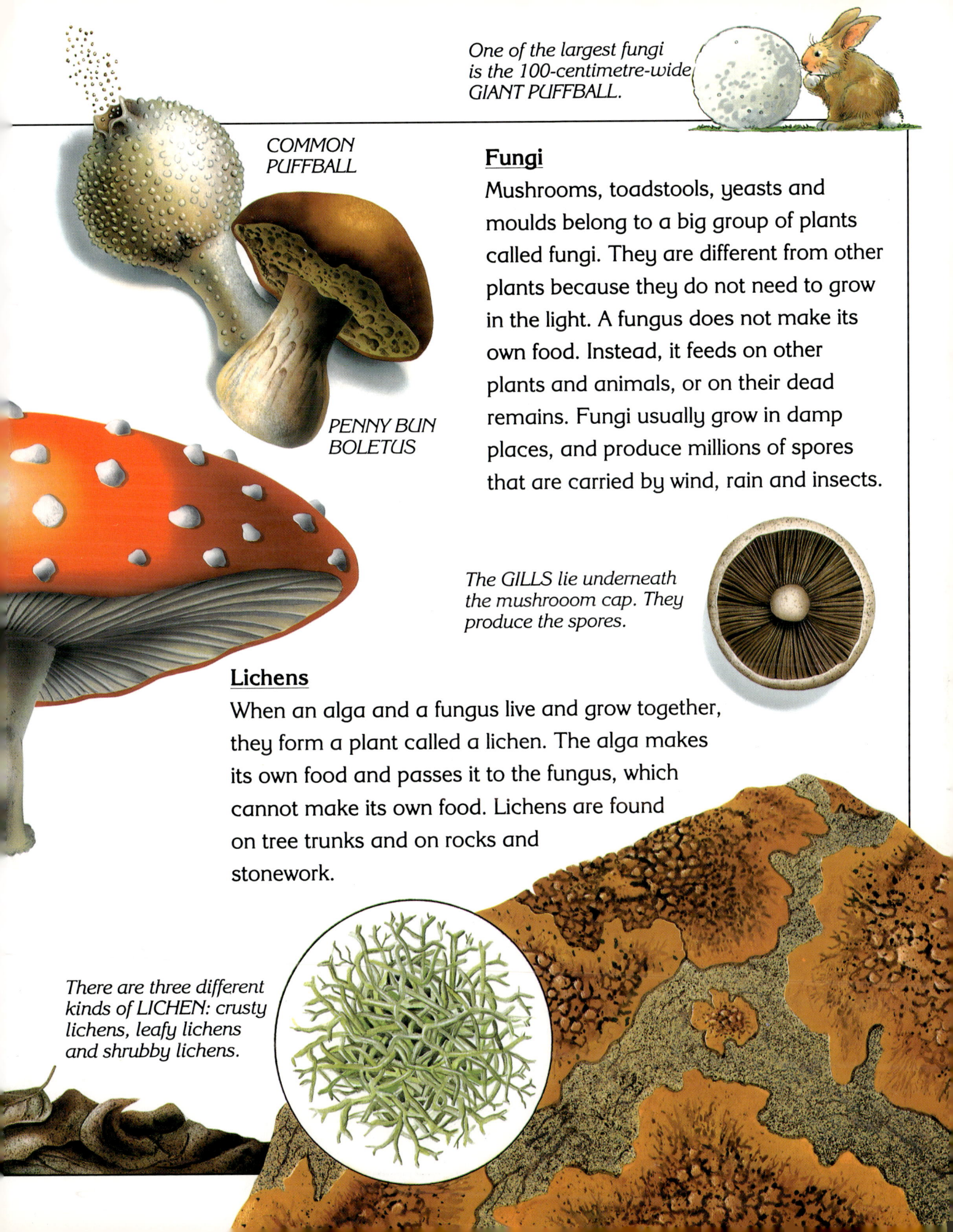

*One of the largest fungi is the 100-centimetre-wide GIANT PUFFBALL.*

COMMON PUFFBALL

PENNY BUN BOLETUS

## Fungi

Mushrooms, toadstools, yeasts and moulds belong to a big group of plants called fungi. They are different from other plants because they do not need to grow in the light. A fungus does not make its own food. Instead, it feeds on other plants and animals, or on their dead remains. Fungi usually grow in damp places, and produce millions of spores that are carried by wind, rain and insects.

*The GILLS lie underneath the mushroom cap. They produce the spores.*

## Lichens

When an alga and a fungus live and grow together, they form a plant called a lichen. The alga makes its own food and passes it to the fungus, which cannot make its own food. Lichens are found on tree trunks and on rocks and stonework.

*There are three different kinds of LICHEN: crusty lichens, leafy lichens and shrubby lichens.*

# FROM SPORES TO NEW PLANTS

*Oarweed*

## Seaweeds
Seaweed algae do not have true stems, leaves or roots. They attach themselves to rocks and other hard surfaces with a structure called a holdfast. Seaweed spores have to join together before a new plant can grow.

*Holdfast*

If you look on the underside of a fern leaf, you will often see small patches or spots. Some are a dull brownish–black colour, but others are bright yellow. These patches are really tiny sacs and they contain the fern's spores. On a dry day, the ripe sacs burst open and the spores float into the air.

*LIVERWORTS grow slowly and are usually no more than 20 centimetres long.*

## Mosses and liverworts
Mosses and liverworts are low–growing plants found in damp places such as bogs, woods and riverbanks. Water helps the male and female cells of the plants to join together, so that spore capsules can begin to develop. The capsules grow on the tips of thin umbrella–like stalks. When they are dry, the spores fall out and are blown away.

*Liverwort umbrella*

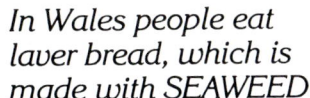

*In Wales people eat laver bread, which is made with SEAWEED.*

*A TREE FERN can grow up to 20 metres high.*

## How do new ferns grow?

Although ferns grow in many different shapes and sizes, they all reproduce in the same way. The fern spores which land in damp, shady areas start to grow into tiny plants. These plants are not the same as the plants that made the spores, but they produce the male and female cells. These cells join together to grow into a mature fern plant.

## Finding fossils

Fossils are the remains of plants and animals that lived on Earth thousands or even millions of years ago. In some cases, the impression of the plant or animal can be seen in layers of rock. Many different fossils have been found – from ferns and fish to insects and dinosaurs.

*Fern fossil*

# PLANT FAMILIES

There are around 350,000 different kinds of plant. Botanists (scientists who study plants) have divided plants into different groups. All the plants in a group are similar to each other. Botanists separate flowering plants into two main groups, depending on the number of seed leaves they grow. Plants in one group have seeds with only one seed leaf. Those in the other group have two seed leaves.

FUNGUS

MOSS

FERN

# KEEPING A RECORD

You can keep a record of different seeds, bulbs and spores by creating your own nature diary. Using a simple exercise book or scrap book, draw pictures and write down information about plants you see, and stick in examples of seeds. If you have a camera, you could even include some photographs.

Remember to write down the name of the plants you have seen, and the place and date when you first saw each one. You may have to look up the names of some plants in a reference book, or ask an adult to help you. Here are just some of the items you may want to record in your diary.

### Sporing mushrooms

Look for mushrooms in woods and in open fields. Don't touch them unless you are sure they are not poisonous ones.
Name of mushroom:
Size and colour:
Where does it grow?:
Can you see spores?:

### What we eat

Look closely at the different food packets in your kitchen cupboards. Read the ingredients labels to find out what's inside each food. Are you surprised how many foods are made from seeds?
Name of food:
From which seed?:
Plant name:

### From flower to fruit:

Collect as many different fruits as you can find. Remember that "fruits" are not just the apples and oranges you eat.
Name of flower:
Kind of fruit:
Hard or fleshy?:
Number of seeds:

### Seeds from trees

In the autumn, you will find lots of tree seeds scattered on the ground. Do you know which trees they come from?
Tree name:
Enclosed or naked seed?:
Seed description:
How is seed spread?:

## Spreading seeds

By looking at the shape of a seed, can you guess how it is spread away from the parent plant?
Shape of seed:
Parent plant:
How is it spread?:

## Pollinators

Take a close look at some colourful flowers on a sunny day. Can you see lots of insects at work?
Name of insect:
Name of flower:
Flower colour:
Is it scented?:
Can you see honey guides?:

## Favourite foods

We have seen some animals which help to spread seeds by eating fruits and nuts. Can you find out the names of other seed–eating animals?

Name of seed:
Which animal eats it?:
How is it collected?:
Is it stored?:

## Lichens

Look for lichens in woodlands, on stones and on brick or stone walls.
Where does it grow?:
Colour:
Which type?:

# MORE AMAZING FACTS

In woodland areas, badgers dig up BLUEBELL bulbs and eat them.

Before each winter, DORMICE eat so many seeds and nuts that their body weight almost doubles.

The dried seeds of the JAMAICAN PEPPER plant are called allspice because they taste of cinnamon, cloves and nutmeg.

The PAPAYA fruit can be rubbed into uncooked meat to make it tender.

The world's most poisonous fungus, the DEATH-CAP, can kill a person who eats it, but rabbits and slugs who do so will come to no harm.

The ripe pods of the TOUCH-ME-NOT throw out seeds when touched.

GRAIN WEEVILS lay their eggs inside grain seeds. Their larvae eat the grain.

Fairy rings of MUSHROOMS on the Great Plains in the US can be 60 metres wide.

# Glossary

**BULB** An underground part of a plant, made of fleshy leaves, that stores food.

**CARPEL** The female part of a flower.

**CEREAL** A grain used as food, such as barley and wheat.

**CONIFER** A tree or shrub that produces cones. Most have needle-shaped leaves.

**CORM** A thick underground stem that stores food.

**DISPERSE** To scatter.

**FERTILISATION** When the male cells of a plant join with the female egg cells so that a new plant can form.

**FLORET** A small flower within a cluster.

**FRONDS** The leaves of a fern.

**FRUIT** Ripe seeds and their surrounding structure. Fruits may be soft like strawberries or hard like acorns.

**HONEY GUIDES** The markings on some flowers which lead insects to the nectar.

**MINERAL** A substance in the soil that helps a plant to grow strong and healthy.

**NECTAR** A sugary liquid that is made inside certain flowers.

**PISTIL** The female part of a flower.

**POLLINATION** The transfer of pollen from the male part to the female part of a flower.

**RHIZOME** A thick storage stem that grows sideways, either along or under the ground, and produces roots and leafy shoots.

**RUNNER** A long stem from the main plant that grows out along the ground and develops roots.

**SEED** The part of a plant that is able to grow into a new plant.

**SPORE** A tiny cell that can develop into a new plant.

**STAMEN** The male part of a flower.

**TUBER** A swollen stem or root that grows underground.

# INDEX

**A**
alga  4, 22, 23, 24, 26

**B**
beans  9, 17
berries  15
botanist  26
bulbils  18
bulbs  5, 18, 19, 30, 31

**C**
capsules  7, 24
carpel  10, 31
cereals  16, 31
classification  26
cones  6, 13, 26
conifers  6, 13, 26, 31
corm  18, 31

**D**
dispersion  14, 15, 31
drinks  17

**E**
egg cells  6, 10, 12
enclosed seeds  6

**F**
female cells  10, 24, 25
ferns  4, 5, 22, 24, 25, 26
fertilisation  12, 31

floret  12
flower head  12
flowering plants  4, 6, 7, 10, 26
fossil  25
fruit  4, 6, 7, 13, 15, 28, 29, 30
fungi  4, 22–26, 30

**H**
honey guides  11, 31

**L**
leaves  5
lichen  4, 23, 26, 29
liverworts  22, 24, 26

**M**
male cells  10, 24, 25
moss  4, 22, 24, 26
mould  22, 26

**N**
naked seeds  6
nectar  11, 31
non-flowering plants  4
nuts  4, 5, 13, 14, 15, 29, 30

**O**
oil  16

**P**
pistil  10, 31
pods  14, 17, 30
pollen  10, 11, 12
pollen baskets  11
pollen grain  11, 12
pollinators  29
pollination  10, 11, 29, 31

**R**
rhizome  20, 31
roots  8, 20, 21
runners  20, 31

**S**
sacs  24
scales  6, 13
seaweed  22, 24, 25, 27
seed coat  8, 9
seed head  14
seed leaves  8, 9
seeds  4, 6-17, 28, 29, 30, 31
shoots  8
spices  16, 17
spores  4, 22–25, 31
stamen  10, 31
stems  18, 20, 21

**T**
tuber  20, 31